101 HARMONICA TIPS

STUFF ALL THE PROS KNOW AND USE

BY STEVE COHEN

ISBN 978-0-61780-604-9

HAL•LEONARD®
7777 W. BLUEMOUND RD. P.O. BOX 13819 MILWAUKEE, WI 53213

In Australia Contact:
Hal Leonard Australia Pty. Ltd.
4 Lentara Court
Cheltenham, Victoria, 3192 Australia
Email: ausadmin@halleonard.com.au

Visit Hal Leonard Online at
www.halleonard.com

INTRODUCTION

The 10-hole diatonic harmonica is a unique instrument. Capable of limitless expression, it is usually learned by ear. This book will help you learn to start playing or improve your playing using a by-ear method, as well as with musical notation and tablature. Also included is practical information relating to performance, maintenance, and the wide world of harmonicas.

ABOUT THE AUTHOR

Steve Cohen, based in Milwaukee, Wisconsin, is a performing musician, a professional educator, and a booking agent. He has been sponsored by Hohner Inc., the world's largest maker of harmonicas, since 1986. He also plays the guitar and sings. Steve performs regularly in several of his own ensembles, averaging more than 100 personal appearances a year and is in demand as a sideman for both local and national groups. He has produced eight published recordings of his own, and his playing has appeared on dozens of other recordings, demos, and commercials as a session player.

Steve has received public recognition, winning over a dozen awards from several organizations, including the Wisconsin Area Music Industry (WAMI), the *Shepherd Express* Readers Poll, and *Milwaukee Magazine*. He was a finalist at the 2010 International Blues Challenge in Memphis as a solo performer.

Steve taught a blues history course at the University of Wisconsin, Milwaukee from 2005–2009. He has also taught harmonica and guitar to many private students. His Blues Central booking agency, the only one in his area devoted to blues and other forms of non-commercial music, has been in operation since the early 1980s. In his thirty-plus year career, other music-related activities have included work as a disc jockey, journalist, concert promoter, and LP and CD dealer.

Steve has also recorded the harmonica parts for numerous Hal Leonard *Harmonica Play-Along* book/audios, as well as a variety of other Hal Leonard products.

Visit Steve online at **www.stevecohenblues.com**.

TABLE OF CONTENTS

1 CHOOSING A MODEL AND BRAND

There are at least a dozen manufacturers offering a wide variety of models of 10-hole diatonic harmonicas. Hohner is still among the most popular brands. If you buy a Hohner to start, I'd recommend a Marine Band, Special 20, or Golden Melody. These models are of professional quality. Some of the other brands that make good harps are Lee Oskar, Hering, Huang, and Sydell.

2 CUSTOM HARPS

There are now craftsmen who make high-quality, custom harps. These harps can be built and set up for your particular needs. Spearheading the movement is Joe Filisko of Joliet, Illinois, but there are several other skilled builders. I use my set of Filisko harps sparingly, usually just for recording or special occasions. They play more easily and sound better than stock harps.

3 CHOOSING A KEY

There are twelve keys, and diatonic harmonicas are manufactured in all twelve. The lowest-pitched stock harp is G, and the highest is F#. The C harp is pitched in the middle, and if you're starting with one harmonica, C would be a good choice, as it is the most neutral. *All demo tracks accompanying this book will be played on a C harp.* Some manufacturers make harps that are tuned extra high, extra low, or with alternate tunings. Low D, low F, and high G are among the most useful of these.

4 WOOD VS. PLASTIC/METAL COMBS

Harmonicas are constructed with a comb in the center, a reed plate on each side of it, and covers on the top and bottom. Combs can be made of different materials. These materials give the instrument characteristics that partially dictate how they sound and play.

Harps with wood combs can swell when they get excess saliva in them. When the wood swells, the teeth in the comb can stick out and create a hazard to your lips. The teeth usually shrink back down, but they don't always go back down all the way, or can shrink too far into the harmonica. Excess saliva is more often a problem for beginners than for more experienced players. Many great players swear by wood-combed models.

Harps with plastic or metal combs don't swell. Wood combs are thought to produce a more mellow tone than harps with plastic or metal combs, and some players prefer wood-combed harps for the tonal quality. The difference is subtle, especially if you are playing with distortion through an amplifier. Different makes and models sound and play differently.

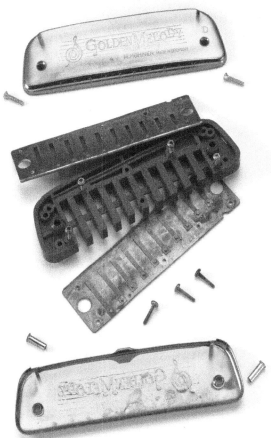

Other differences between makes and models concern the size of the holes, the size and shape of the reed plate covers, and the ease with which one can repair them. Some harps have replaceable reed plates, while others have replaceable reeds. There are many options and a wide price range, soaring to hundreds of dollars per harp. It is best to try different models and get a feel for which is best for you.

STANCE

Find a comfortable way to hold your harmonica. With the numbers facing up, put it in the crook of your left hand between your index finger and your thumb. Put your thumb straight up at a right angle to the harp so that the back of your thumb touches the front of the harp without blocking the first hole. Do the same with your right hand, trying not to block the 10 hole, and then fold your hands around the back of the instrument until they meet and create a seal. This forms a little cup of air between the harp and the back of your hands.

Posture is important. If you are sitting, sit up straight. If you are standing, stand up straight. Your ability to maximize your breathing is what powers the notes. Breathe deeply, from your diaphragm.

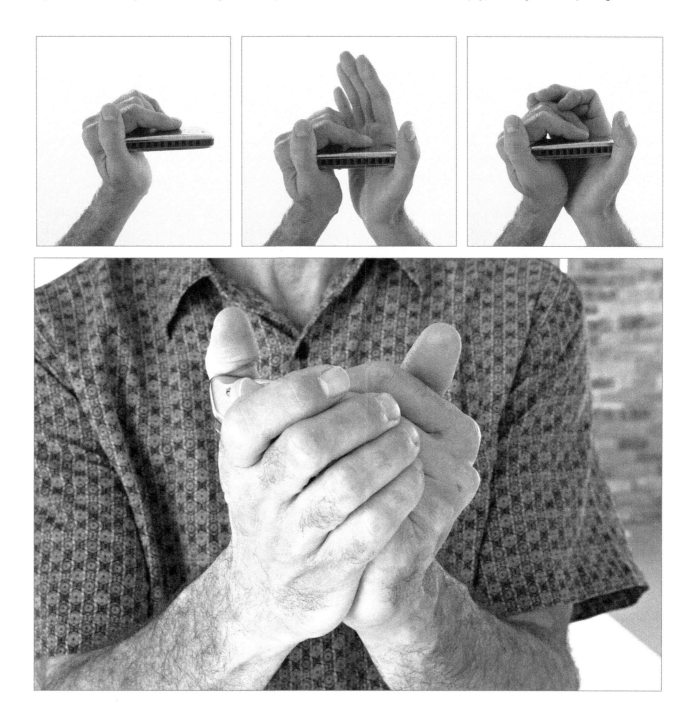

Rest the bottom of the harp on the inside of your lower lip, and then close your lips around it. Your lips should be firm but relaxed enough for the harp to slide. The same goes for the way your hands hold the harp—firm, but not in a death grip. Hold the harp parallel to the ground, not at an angle. The harmonica should sit as deep in your mouth as is comfortable. Be sure that none of the air going through the harmonica is leaking where the instrument meets your mouth. If you are getting weak notes or can hear air leaking, adjust how the harp meets your mouth.

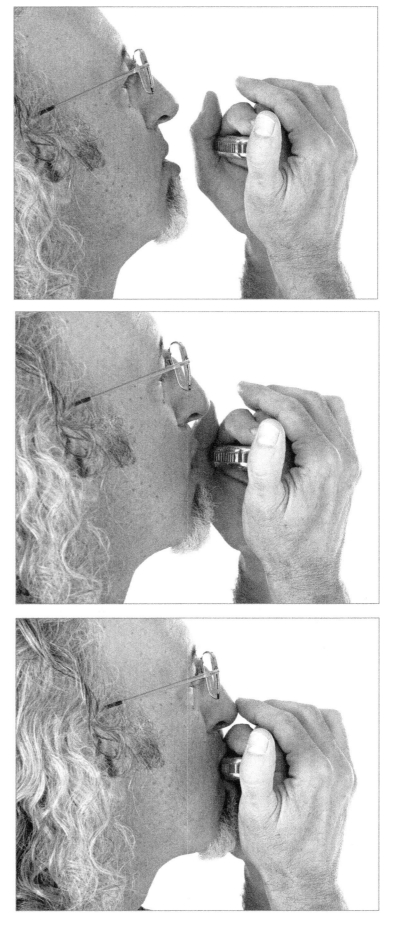

7 BLUES LICK #1: CHORDS

Here's an easy blues lick. Blues Lick #1 is the harmonica equivalent of a familiar guitar shuffle rhythm. Play it with two- or three-note chords here.

This lick also makes a nice starting point for an *a cappella* harp jam. Listen, and then play it over the solo guitar accompaniment in track 2.

Blues Lick #1

TRACK 1

Without Harp

TRACK 2

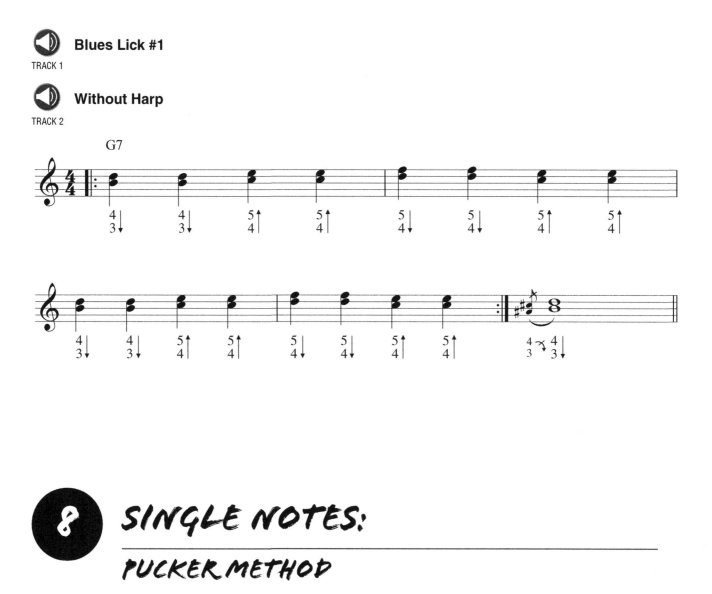

8 SINGLE NOTES:
PUCKER METHOD

Being able to isolate single notes is an important basic skill. Using the pucker method, form your lips as though you are drinking through a straw. With the harp in your mouth, create a small opening where your lips meet—just big enough to play one hole at a time—through which air is then pushed or pulled through the reed. Using this method, it is possible to play with a great deal of speed, even when bending notes.

9 · SINGLE NOTES:

TONGUE BLOCKING

Using this method, your tongue blocks the holes to the left of the note you want to play, while the right corner of your lips blocks the notes to the right of the note you want to play. This method produces a more complex tone. Tongue blocking makes it possible to alternate between high and low notes, and also to produce chords and octaves made up of notes that are not adjacent. I think of this method as more difficult for bending, but bending with tongue blocking is still doable. I play both ways, but for the early examples I suggest using the pucker method.

10 · SINGLE NOTES:

GETTING STARTED

Using the pucker method, start by trying to get a clean, strong, single note on hole 1, draw and blow.

TRACK 3

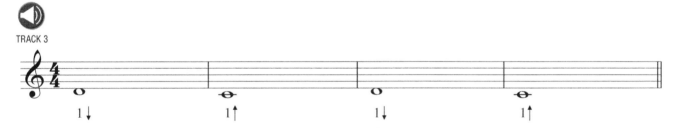

1↓   1↑   1↓   1↑

Next, starting with the 1 hole, pucker up and run all the way up the harp using draw notes, then run all the way down. Do this again using blow notes.

TRACK 4

Next, do it again, but more slowly. Give all the notes the same time value and an individual identity.

TRACK 5

11 BLUES LICK #1:

SINGLE NOTES

Try Blues Lick #1 again, this time with single notes instead of chords:

TRACK 6

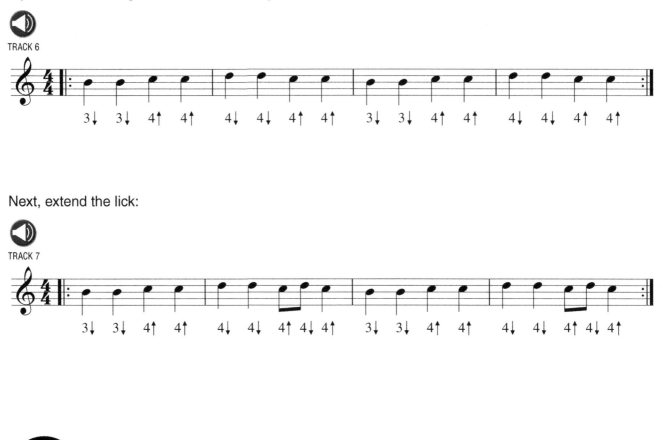

Next, extend the lick:

TRACK 7

12 EQUALIZING INHALE AND EXHALE

The harmonica is the only instrument from which you get notes by both inhaling and exhaling. If you repeat an extended lick several times without stopping to take a breath, you will run out of air. Invariably, notes in any phrase will be made up of more draw notes or more blow notes. There is a valve in the back of your nose that will reflexively open and close to help you equalize the natural breathing pattern that is part of playing the harmonica. But, you'll also need to find spots while playing where you can take an extra breath, or release a breath without compromising your phrasing.

13 POSITIONS – BACKGROUND

The music in this book so far that you've been playing on your C harp is actually in the key of G or 2nd position. Another name for 2nd position is *cross harp*. Because the harmonica does not readily contain the entire chromatic scale, different positions are used for songs that have different melodic orientations.

There are four positions that are generally considered, and commonly used, called 1st, 2nd, 3rd, and 4th position. You can usually play one of these four positions more easily than the others throughout a particular song. A song's key and scale orientation will determine which position it will be most easily played on. It may be possible to play a particular song with more than one position, but it will involve less bending acrobatics if you figure out which position is easiest for the song at hand.

There are actually twelve positions. I know of only one harmonica player who can make a meaningful statement in all twelve keys on one harp. So for most of us, this is theoretical. The concept, however, illustrates how we think of playing different harmonicas over different keys.

As an example, if you were able to play the example in Tip #14 ("Oh! Susanna") in all four positions, it would soon become clear that 3rd and 4th position involve excessive and prohibitive bending and register jumping. Furthermore, the chord changes of this song move from the I chord to the V chord, which would make 1st position the most logical choice. There is further explanation in Tip #14.

1ST POSITION

STRAIGHT HARP

1st position is sometimes referred to as *straight harp*. The harmonica was originally designed to be played over chord progressions that moved from the I chord to the V chord. In 1st position, the blow notes all sound good over the I chord, and the draw notes all sound good over the V chord. This position works well for folk music, campfire songs, Christmas songs, and other styles of music that use mainly major scales. There are also some applications for blues, jazz, and rock playing. This is the position often used by guys like Bob Dylan and Neil Young.

In this position, the high notes contain a number of bends that increase the chromatic possibilities, but jumping from the bottom of the harp to a higher octave may sound clumsy or contrived. There are a handful of songs recorded in the late 1920s by an artist called Blues Birdhead, whose high-note work maximizes the chromatic possibilities of the high-note bends in a jazz format.

🔊 "Oh! Susanna" in 1st Position

TRACK 8

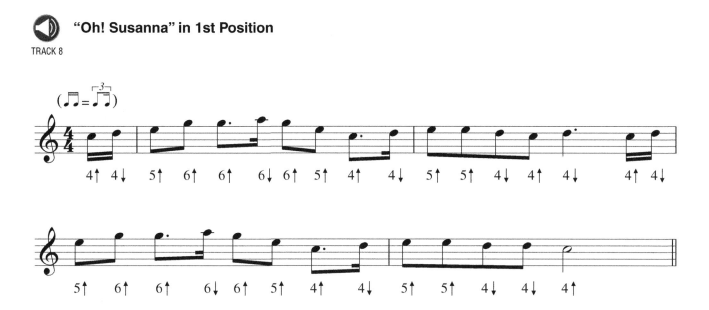

15 2ND POSITION

CROSS HARP

Cross harp is the position that is typically used to play blues, jazz, and rock music. In this position, the key of the harmonica is four scale steps up from the key of the song. Playing a C harp in the key of G, or an A harp in the key of E are examples. In 2nd position, the draw notes work well over the I chord, and the blow notes work well over the IV chord. In the early 1900s, someone discovered that the number of available chromatic notes increased over blues changes when using 2nd position, and it became a popular way of playing. This position has more chromatic possibilities on the low end of the harp than does 1st position, partially because of the scale orientation, and partially because of how bending low notes fills in some of the chromatic gaps.

🔊 **"Oh! Susanna" in 2nd Position**

TRACK 9

15

16 3RD POSITION

3rd position is four scale steps up from 2nd position, or a scale step lower than the key of the song. An example would be playing a C harp in the key of D. The available notes in this position correspond more readily to minor-pitched songs than 1st or 2nd positions.

"Oh! Susanna" in 3rd Position

TRACK 10

4TH POSITION

In 4th position, one uses a harmonica that is another four scale steps up from a 3rd-position harp, such as playing a C harp in the key of A. This position also works well for certain minor-pitched tunes. Bob Dylan used this position on his original recording of "All Along the Watchtower."

"Oh! Susanna" in 4th Position

TRACK 11

Though you probably won't need more than the first four positions, here is a guide which includes all twelve positions:

Position/ Harp Key	1st Major	2nd Mixolydian	3rd Dorian	4th Aeolian	5th Phrygian	6th Locrian	7th	8th	9th	10th	11th	12th Lydian
C	C	G	D	A	E	B	F#/Gb	Db	Ab	Eb	Bb	F
G	G	D	A	E	B	F#/Gb	Db	Ab	Eb	Bb	F	C
D	D	A	E	B	F#/Gb	Db	Ab	Eb	Bb	F	C	G
A	A	E	B	F#/Gb	Db	Ab	Eb	Bb	F	C	G	D
E	E	B	F#/Gb	Db	Ab	Eb	Bb	F	C	G	D	A
B	B	F#/Gb	Db	Ab	Eb	Bb	F	C	G	D	A	E
F#/Gb	F#/Gb	Db	Ab	Eb	Bb	F	C	G	D	A	E	B
Db	Db	Ab	Eb	Bb	F	C	G	D	A	E	B	F#/Gb
Ab	Ab	Eb	Bb	F	C	G	D	A	E	B	F#/Gb	Db
Eb	Eb	Bb	F	C	G	D	A	E	B	F#/Gb	Db	Ab
Bb	Bb	F	C	G	D	A	E	B	F#/Gb	Db	Ab	Eb
F	F	C	G	D	A	E	B	F#/Gb	Db	Ab	Eb	Bb

Second position (cross harp) is the most-used position and is highlighted in the chart. Indicated also is the major key or modes that some of the positions represent.

18 BENDING THE LOW NOTES

Of the twelve notes next to each other in the chromatic musical scale, several notes don't naturally exist on the harp. A key of C harp played in the key of C has only the white keys of the piano, none of the black keys. However, some of the missing notes can be reached by bending. This makes learning and mastering bends an important technique. All of the bends on the low end of the harp (holes 1–6) are achieved by drawing, and each bend lowers the pitch a half step. See Tip #50 for more information on high-note bends. Also, there are larger bends possible on holes 2 and 3.

Here is a chart of where all the bends are located on the harp:

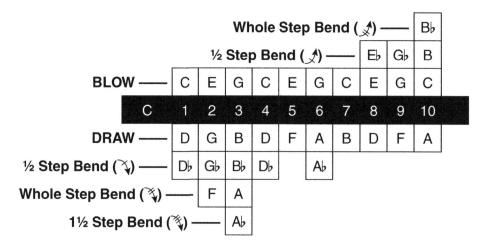

Hole 5 can be bent, but it doesn't quite bend down a half step to E.

19 HOW TO BEND

If you are not getting strong, clean, single notes, you will not be able to bend, so be sure you are getting all the air through the reed.

It's challenging to describe how notes are physically bent because the harmonica is the only instrument in which the mechanism that produces notes is entirely hidden from view. Your embouchure must change when moving from a natural to a bent note. The term *embouchure* refers to the configuration of the muscles in your mouth. When bending notes, you are changing the vowel shape of your mouth. While inhaling, try saying "wee-oh." Then try it with a harp in your mouth while playing a 1 or 4 draw. What happens in your mouth when you bend? Your jaw drops and moves forward a little, and your tongue follows the depressed shape of your mouth. Bending can be difficult when starting out, but with persistence, a note will eventually bend for you. On your C harp, the 1 and 4 holes will probably bend the easiest, but try bending all holes 1–6.

20 BENDING EXERCISES

These exercises can be a big help in locating the bent notes, as well as in achieving proficiency at bending. It is easier to bend down from an unbent note than to hit a bent note cold. These exercises involve bending from both directions.

TRACK 12

21 THE IN-BETWEEN NOTES

A special characteristic of the harmonica comes to light when you start bending. Since we're changing notes by bending without a fret, key, or valve, we're able to play through some notes that are "in between" the notes of the scales. The good news is that this gives the harmonica a vocal quality that is very desirable. The bad news is that it makes it all the more imperative to hit the bent notes accurately in order to play in tune.

22 HOLD THOSE BENDS

Getting proficient at bending notes can be accelerated by holding the bent note as long as possible without losing the integrity of the pitch. By doing this, you are developing both stamina and muscle memory. Muscle memory is important here, because each bend has a slightly different embouchure. If you play another instrument, you may want to check the accuracy of your bent notes against the same notes on your other instrument at first.

TRACK 13

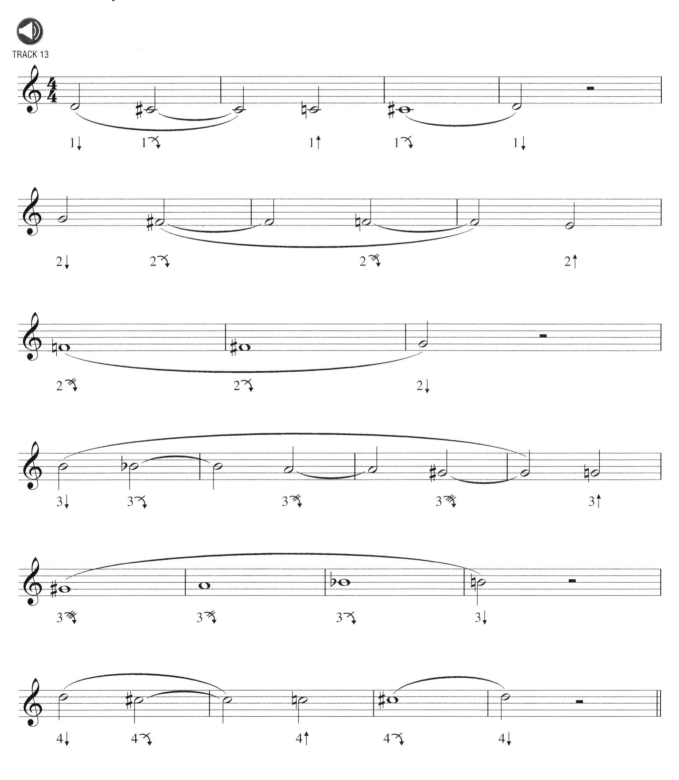

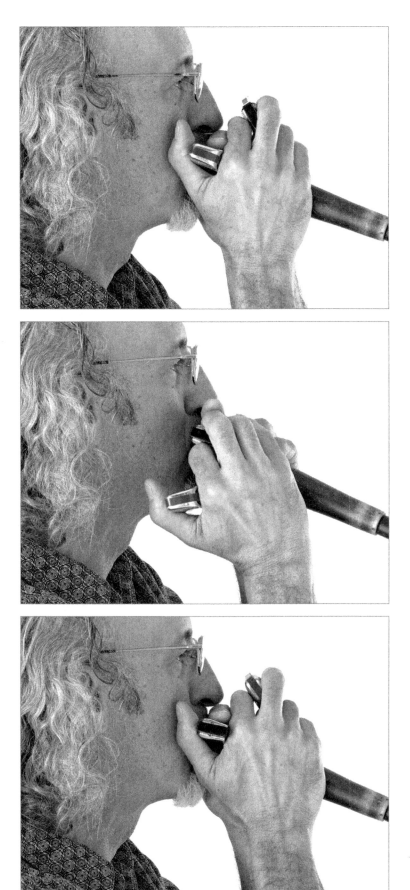

Sometimes the easiest way to play over certain chord changes in a song is by switching harps. This can be helpful in a song that changes keys, or has a bridge in a different key than the verses. While you are playing one harp, you can have the next one ready between your second and third fingers, and even a third harp between your third and fourth fingers.

Some popular songs that use this technique are "Orange Blossom Special," and the original Kris Kristofferson version of "Me and Bobby McGee."

24 OVERBLOWING & OVERDRAWING

Just as cross harp and note bending were discovered and incorporated long after the invention of the instrument, so has overblowing been added to the techniques that assist in completing a chromatic approach to diatonic harp playing.

In 1969, harp player and keyboard artist Howard Levy discovered that by overbending the low notes upward via blowing and overbending the high notes upward via drawing, the complete chromatic scale became available on the 10-hole diatonic harmonica.

This is achieved (much like bending) with a different set of embouchures. An overblowing embouchure is similar to that which is used in high-note bending. An overdrawing embouchure is similar to that used in low-note bending.

Although this book will not go further with instruction in this technique, it's good to be aware of the new possibilities. Here are a few examples of overblowing.

TRACK 14

(25) BLUES CHANGES

Much American popular music is played over various combinations of I, IV, and V chords. These are also the chord changes to a majority of blues tunes, and are called "blues changes" when played in certain sequences. Being able to navigate over these changes is an integral part of harmonica playing.

The 12-Bar Form

The *12-bar form* is common to the largest number of blues songs. At its most basic, it consists of three specific elements:

a. **Timing:** 12 bars

b. **Chord Relationship:** I, IV, V

c. **Lyric Structure:** AAB lyric form

A *bar* (or measure) is a segment of time defined by a given number of beats (in this case four) in equal time: 1-2-3-4. Twelve of these bars equal one verse. Once completed, the cycle repeats. Several repetitions are contained in a song.

TRACK 15

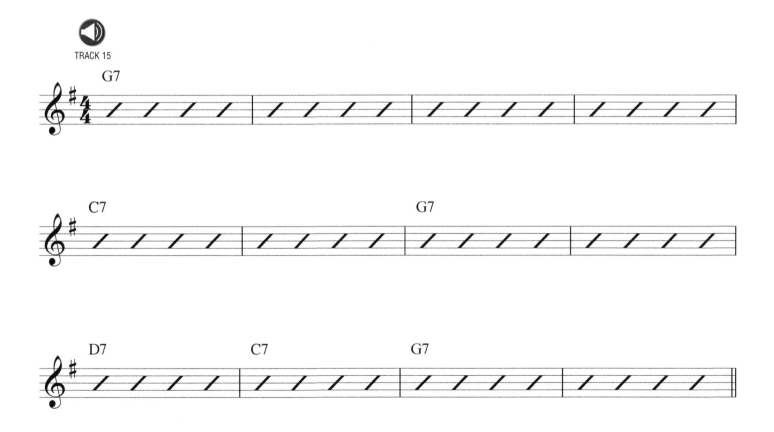

24

Each of these individual twelve bars gets assigned a specific chord or chords, and a pattern or progression of chord changes is created. Blues changes are based on the I, IV, and V chords. If we look at the diagram of scale steps and Roman numeral chord symbols below, you can see how we arrive at these chords:

Scale step:	1	2	3	4	5	6	7
Note name:	G	A	B	C	D	E	F
Chord degree:	I			IV	V		

If the key of the song is G, we assign the Roman numeral I to the letter G, it is the root note of the I chord (the *root* is the fundamental note of a chord or scale). Next, including the G, we count forward, or up four scale steps to the letter C, which is the root note of the IV chord. Next, from the G, count forward five scale steps. We arrive at the letter D. D is the root note of the V chord.

26 BASIC BLUES PROGRESSION

Here is a diagram of a basic 12-bar blues progression:

Bar count:	1	2	3	4	5	6	7	8	9	10	11	12
Chord name:	G	G	G	G	C	C	G	G	D	C	G	G
Chord degree:	I	I	I	I	IV	IV	I	I	V	IV	I	I

27 PLAYING OVER BLUES CHANGES

On the 10-hole diatonic harp (pitched in C), the note G, the root of the I chord, may be played four ways: 2↓, 3↑, 6↑, 9↑

TRACK 16

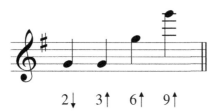

2↓ 3↑ 6↑ 9↑

The note C, the root of the IV chord, can be played four ways: 1↑, 4↑, 7↑, 10↑

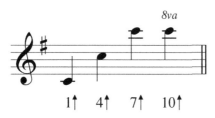

1↑ 4↑ 7↑ 10↑

The note D, the root of the V chord, can be played three ways: 1↓, 4↓, 8↓

1↓ 4↓ 8↓

Here is a basic 12-bar played with only three notes of the harmonica. Each of the three notes corresponds to the I, IV, or V chords of a 12-bar blues:

 With Harp

TRACK 17

 Without Harp

TRACK 18

28 COMMON 12-BAR VARIATIONS

There are many variations of the 12-bar form. The two most common variations are shown here...

With a IV chord in the second bar, and a V chord for the 12th bar:

With Harp

TRACK 19

Without Harp

TRACK 20

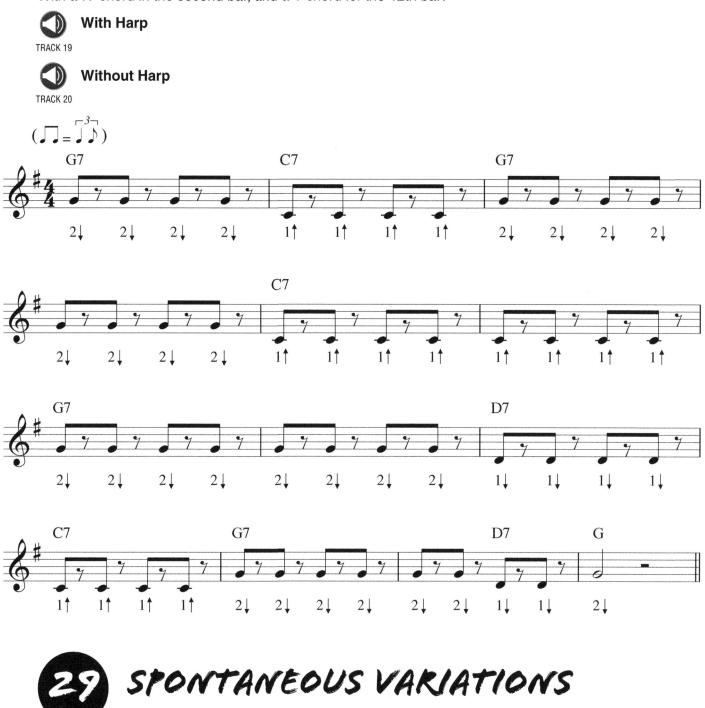

29 SPONTANEOUS VARIATIONS

Here is a word of warning about 12-bar blues progressions in the real world. Traditional blues musicians sometimes customize these rules by spontaneously adding or subtracting a half a bar, a bar, two bars, or whatever they feel like at any point in a progression. This is legitimate and authentic blues playing. Sometimes chord changes are hinted at in the vocal melody, but the accompaniment doesn't change. As an accompanist, you are expected to always be listening and able to adjust to these spontaneous variations. Listen to Lightnin' Hopkins or John Lee Hooker for good examples of free-form blues.

30 TURNAROUNDS

Another element of the 12-bar form is the *turnaround*. This is the place at the end of a 12-bar blues progression where a musical phrase over the I chord links the body of the verse to the end of the verse. The following turnaround examples start at bar 8 of a 12-bar progression.

Here's how a turnaround sounds on guitar:

TRACK 21

Here are some turnaround examples on harmonica:

TRACK 22

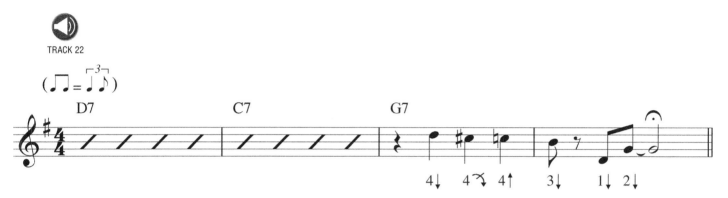

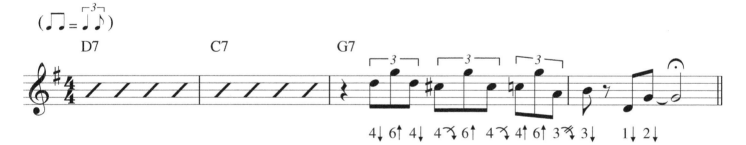

31 SOLOING OVER BLUES CHANGES

Once you are familiar with the 12-bar form, one good way to start soloing is to begin and end your phrases with the note that corresponds to the chord being played. In 2nd position, all draw notes sound good over the I chord, and all blow notes sound good over the IV chord. This, in addition to developing a mixed bag of licks and phrases that can be plugged into your solos, is a good way to start building a solo style.

32 RULES OF ACCOMPANIMENT

The term *comping* (short for "accompany") is defined as playing complimentary phrases or chords behind a singer or soloist. When accompanying a singer, play very little, or not at all during the singing. Wait for the spaces in between the vocal lines. Listen to the singer, and make your response phrases relate to the singer's phrasing. If there is another solo instrument answering the singer, don't play at all. It is important to listen to the other instruments in the ensemble. Do not just wail away, or your presence will be less than desirable.

33 BE READY FOR ANY KEY

Songs with vocals are usually pitched in particular keys to accommodate and maximize the range of the singer's voice. At some point, you'll likely want to have a complete set of twelve harps in anticipation of having to play "Stormy Monday" in A♭ or "Sweet Home Chicago" in F♯.

Also, sometimes guitar players tune down a half or whole step. Be ready for anything.

34 ACCOMPANYING WITH CHORDS

At times, you can provide some chord background to a singer or soloist by playing a wash. A *wash* is a held out chord in the background, sounding much like an organ. Be careful to add to the ensemble sound, and not dominate while playing background parts. It's better to be subtle.

In 2nd position, any combination of draw notes forms a harmonious-sounding background over the I chord. The lower notes will usually conflict less with the vocals than the high register. Likewise, in 2nd position, any combination of blow notes forms a harmonious-sounding background over the IV chord, but the lower notes will be less conflicting with the vocals. You may have noticed that the V chord only appears for one bar or so in a 12-bar, so using a single note or octave is appropriate in that spot, and it passes by quickly.

Here is how this sounds:

TRACK 23

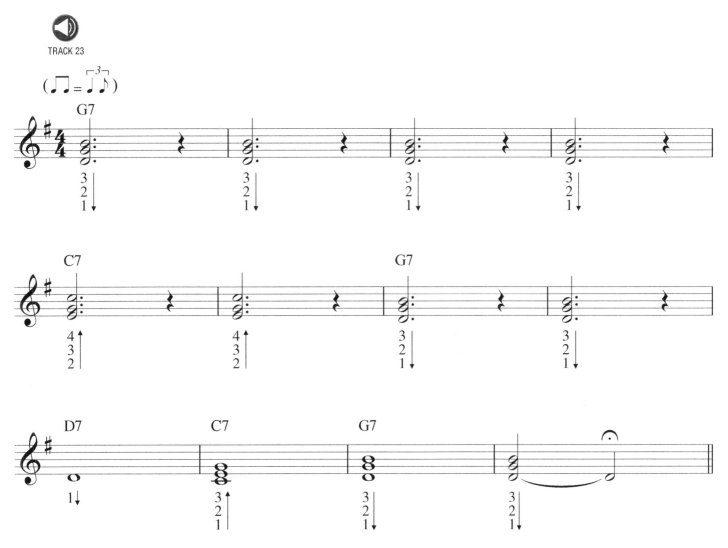

35 MORE COMPING TIPS

Another way to effectively support a singer or soloist is to chop off your chords or single notes rhythmically, with one chop to each beat. Sometimes referred to as "chugging," this is using the harmonica more as a percussion instrument than a melodic one, and is similar to the way other rhythm instruments comp.

TRACK 24

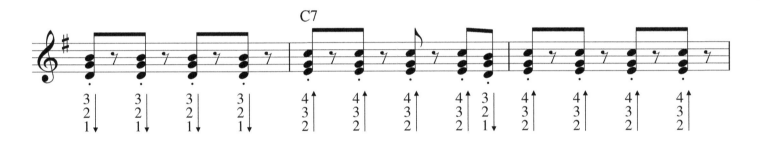

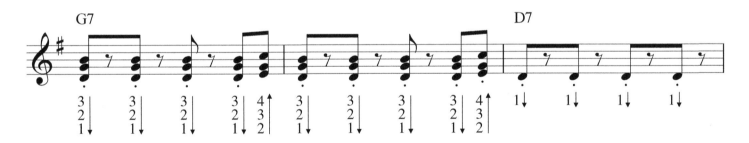

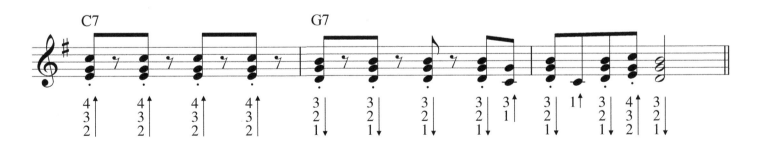

32

12-BAR BLUES LYRIC FORM

It's important to understand how lyrics fit over a 12-bar progression, because harp players often accompany vocals, if not sing them. Many blues lyrics employ the AAB vocal form. Let's call the first line of a verse, A. This vocal line is repeated, sometimes with some variation, as the second A line. The third line, B, usually, but not always, rhymes with the A line. Each line is delivered over four bars. So, the first A line covers bars 1–4, the second A covers bars 5–8, and the B line covers bars 9–12.

Here's how the AAB pattern would look in a 12-bar chart:

Bar count:	1	2	3	4	/	5	6	7	8	/	9	10	11	12
Corresponding chords:	G	G	G	G	/	C	C	G	G	/	D	C	G	G
AAB lyric form:		**A**			/		**A**			/		**B**		

The lyrics of these lines often fill up only two bars or so, usually with an instrumental response filling the other two bars. This is known as "call and response." Track 24 is an example of an AAB blues verse with call-and-response harp accompaniment. Give a listen, and then try playing call-and-response style over track 25.

A: I   "I woke up this morning with a throbbing in my head."

A: IV   "I woke up this morning with a throbbing in my head." **I**

B: V   "I pulled the covers up and **IV** then I went back to **I** bed."

37 LISTEN UP!

It is important to listen to other harp players and learn from them. Little Walter, Sonny Boy Williamson (I & II), Big Walter, Jimmy Reed, James Cotton, Junior Wells, Sonny Terry, Charlie McCoy, DeFord Bailey, and Howard Levy are among the best. There are many other great harp players that are worth a listen; be sure to seek them out. Youtube.com is a great resource. It is also a good idea to build a CD, MP3, or vinyl library as a reference source.

38 DON'T LIMIT YOURSELF

Learn a great guitar song like "Hide Away," or a great sax tune like "Now's the Time." Learning the sax solo from "Honky Tonk" is as valuable as learning harp licks. One aspect of seminal harpist Little Walter's genius was his natural ability to transmute saxophone phrasing into his harp style. He was influenced by jazz greats like Louis Jordan and Gene Ammons.

39 DON'T GET STUCK

Don't get stuck in the trap of only being able to play like someone else. Emulating great harp players is a means to an end. Your long-term goal should be to sound like *you*. There is so much subtlety to the instrument that it is hard to sound exactly like someone else anyway.

 40 OPEN-MINDED EARS

There's a world of music out there, and the harmonica is not limited to one genre. There are great examples of blues, jazz, country, folk, rock, classical, pop, world music, and hip hop harp playing out there. Even if you are only interested in playing one style, there is great value in absorbing elements of other styles.

 41 PRACTICE

Practice is the only way to improve. There is no other way. Budget some time every day to practice. Work on scales, learn classic solos, or pick out a melody you want to learn. If you listen to recordings of yourself practicing, you will get a realistic assessment of how you truly sound.

If you are learning by ear, it's helpful to at least partially memorize the harp part that you are emulating before attempting to execute it. Everyone learns at different rates, so don't get discouraged if you aren't improving quickly enough. Be patient and persistent.

 42 LEARNING DIFFICULT PASSAGES

Learn a system of tablature. Listen to tough phrases in small sections. Chart them out note by note if you need to. Use your player's pause button to help isolate tricky parts. Listen, identify, duplicate, chart it out, and then move on to the next section.

When you've got the whole passage charted out, learn to play it slowly. Once you are accustomed to the phrase, play it a little more quickly until you can play it at the right speed. If you learn to play these sections even quicker than needed, they will play like butter when you execute them at the right speed.

43 GET A LESSON

You can become a better player by getting a hands-on lesson from an experienced player. Find a good teacher and get the benefit of his or her experience. Don't limit yourself to one teacher, as different teachers have different things to offer. The single most important thing I ever did for my playing was to get one lesson from harmonica innovator Howard Levy. It opened doors for me even after I'd already been playing for 15 years. Howard's discovery and mastery of new techniques like overblowing have elevated the harmonica to the status of an instrument equal to any other, superior in some ways. And my short lesson with him moved my playing forward.

44 TRIPLETS

Here are a few triplet rhythms that are good for building facility, practicing bends, and can also be used as elements of soloing:

TRACK 27

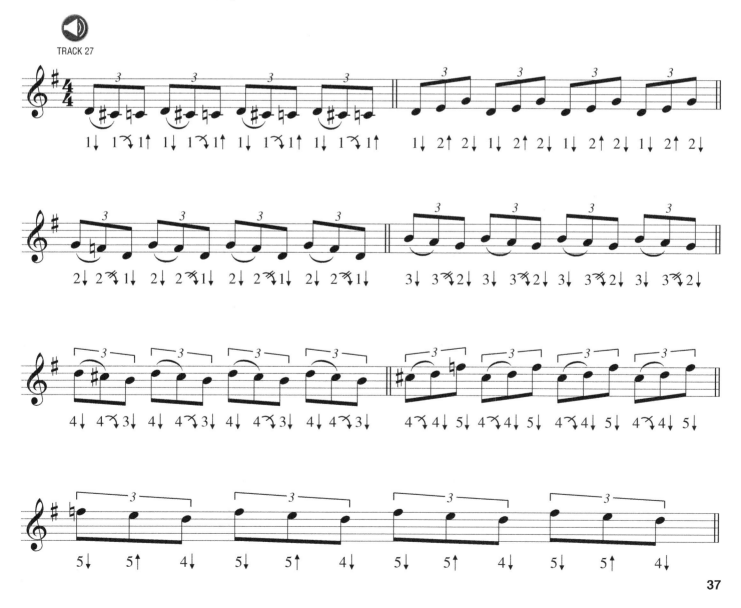

45 THE "HOOCHIE COOCHIE MAN" LICK

The "stop time" lick in this Muddy Waters song is a cornerstone of blues and rock music. "Stop time" means that there are rhythmic stops in a song.

There are many ways to play this lick. The first three examples on track 28 are in 2nd position in the key of G. The fourth example is played like Little Walter played it on the original recording in 1st position. It will be in the key of C in that example. There are many songs where we hear this lick or variations of it.

TRACK 28

46 THE SONNY BOY LICK

This is a famous Sonny Boy Williamson II lick that almost every blues harp player learns. It's really just a triplet with an extra bent note:

TRACK 29

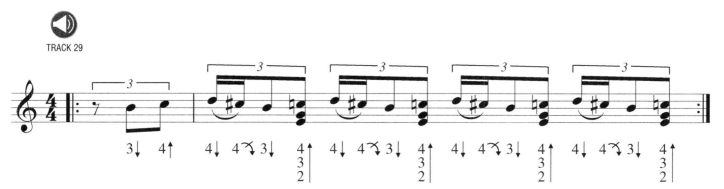

④⑦ LEARN SOME BASS PARTS

Learning some blues bass parts over basic 12-bar blues progressions is a good way to develop more raw materials for soloing and comping.

 Boogie Woogie

TRACK 30

 Without Harp

TRACK 31

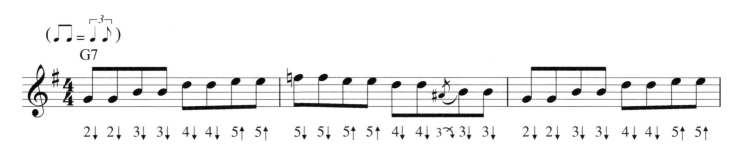

2↓ 2↓ 3↓ 3↓ 4↓ 4↓ 5↑ 5↑   5↓ 5↓ 5↑ 5↑ 4↓ 4↓ 3⤸ 3↓ 3↓   2↓ 2↓ 3↓ 3↓ 4↓ 4↓ 5↑ 5↑

5↓ 5↓ 5↑ 5↑ 4↓ 4↓ 3↓   1↑ 1↑ 2↑ 2↑ 2↓ 2↓ 3⤸3⤸   3⤸3⤸3⤸3⤸3⤸2↓ 2↓ 2↑ 2↑

2↓ 2↓ 3↓ 3↓ 4↓ 4↓ 5↑ 5↑   5↓ 5↓ 5↑ 5↑ 4↓ 4↓ 3↓ 3↓   1↓ 1↓ 2⤸2⤸3⤸3⤸3↓ 3↓

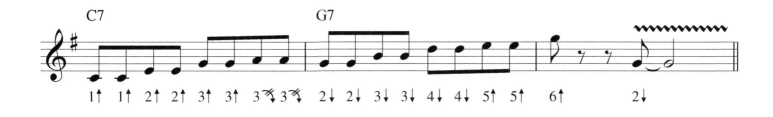

1↑ 1↑ 2↑ 2↑ 3↑ 3↑ 3⤸3⤸   2↓ 2↓ 3↓ 3↓ 4↓ 4↓ 5↑ 5↑ 6↑   2↓

Latin-Flavored Blues

Without Harp

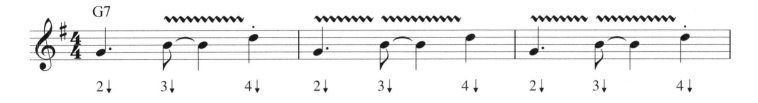

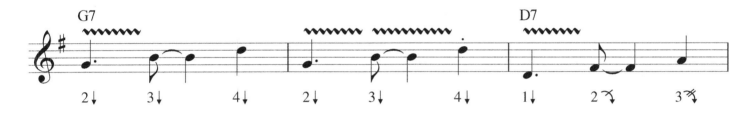

2↓ 2↓ 6↑ 6↑ 5↓ 5↓ 4↓ 4↓   2↓ 2↓ 6↑ 6↑ 5↓ 5↓ 4↓ 4↓   2↓ 2↓ 6↑ 6↑ 5↓ 5↓ 4↓ 4↓

2↓ 2↓ 6↑ 6↑ 5↓ 5↓ 4↓ 4↓   1↑ 1↑ 4↑ 4↑ 3⤹3⤹2↓ 2↓   1↑ 1↑ 4↑ 4↑ 3⤹3⤹2↓

2↓ 2↓ 6↑ 6↑ 5↓ 5↓ 4↓ 4↓   2↓ 2↓ 6↑ 6↑ 5↓ 5↓ 4↓ 4↓   1↓ 1↓ 4↓ 4↓ 4↑ 4↑ 3⤹3⤹

1↑ 1↑ 4↑ 4↑ 3⤹3⤹2↓   2↓ 2↓ 6↑ 6↑ 5↓ 5↓ 4↓ 4↓   2↓   2↓

48 DOUBLE AND TRIPLE TONGUING

Use your tongue to create double- or triple-note rhythms. Try saying "little little" while playing single notes to create a two-note sound, or "diddleup diddleup" for a three-note version. You are using your tongue to interrupt the air stream that powers the notes.

You can practice this technique using the first line of the boogie-woogie pattern. Playing with this technique over the entire song will also help you sharpen up your bending technique.

TRACK 36

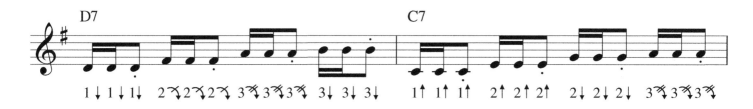

SCALES AND INTERVALS

Practicing some scales and intervals can also help develop facility. There are three registers that cover three octaves on the diatonic harmonica. The relationship of the notes change in each of these three different registers. Playing descending or ascending intervals can help clarify your understanding of the differences between registers:

Four-Note Descending Intervals

TRACK 40

10↓ 9↑ 9↓ 8↑ 9↓ 9↓ 8↑ 8↓ 9↓ 8↑ 8↓ 7↑ 8↑ 8↓ 7↑ 7↓   8↓ 7↑ 7↓ 6↓ 7↑ 7↓ 6↓ 6↑ 7↓ 6↓ 6↑ 5↓ 6↓ 6↑ 5↓ 5↑

6↑ 5↓ 5↑ 4↓ 5↓ 5↑ 4↓ 4↑ 5↑ 4↓ 4↑ 3↓ 4↓ 4↑ 3↓ 3↘

4↑ 3↓ 3↘ 2↓ 3↓ 3↘ 2↓ 2↘ 3↑ 2↓ 2↘ 2↑ 2↓ 2↘ 2↑ 1↓   2↘ 2↑ 1↓ 2↑ 1↑

"Bag's Groove" Lick

TRACK 41

6↑ 6↑ 5↓ 4↓ 5↓ 5↓ 4↓ 4↑ 4↓ 4↓ 4↑ 3↘ 4↑ 4↑ 3↘ 2↓   3↘ 3↘ 2↓ 2↘ 2↓ 2↓ 2↘ 1↓ 2↘ 2↘ 1↓ 1↑ 1↓

"Bag's Groove" Lick Backwards

TRACK 42

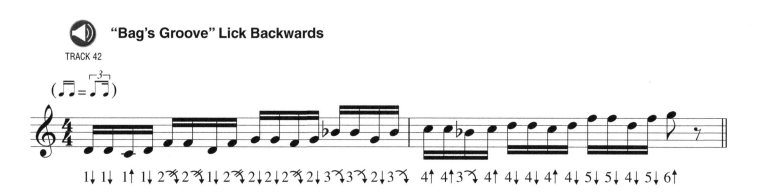

1↓ 1↓ 1↑ 1↓ 2↘ 2↘ 1↓ 2↘ 2↓ 2↓ 2↘ 2↓ 3↘ 3↘ 2↓ 3↘   4↑ 4↑ 3↘ 4↑ 4↓ 4↓ 4↑ 4↓ 5↓ 5↓ 4↓ 5↓ 6↑

Liban Interval

TRACK 43

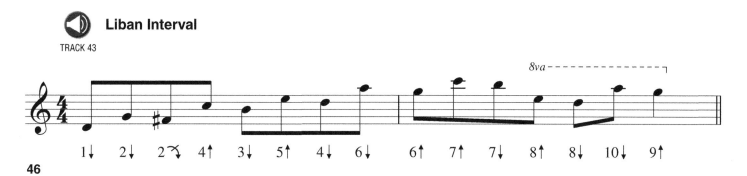

1↓   2↓   2↘   4↑   3↓   5↑   4↓   6↓   6↑   7↑   7↓   8↑   8↓   10↓   9↑

50 HIGH-NOTE BENDS

High notes are bent by blowing, and like low-note bends, the pitch movement goes down a half step for each bend. These bends increase the chromatic possibilities. This requires a different embouchure than low-note bending.

Try saying "tee-oo" to change vowel shape. The 8 hole will be easiest to bend on a C harp. Bends will be easier on a harp pitched lower than C, but they are doable on a C harp.

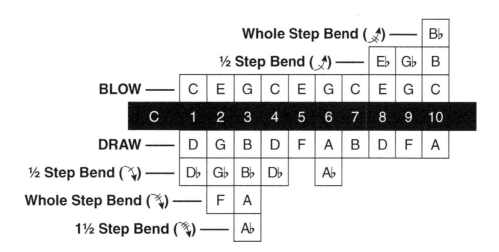

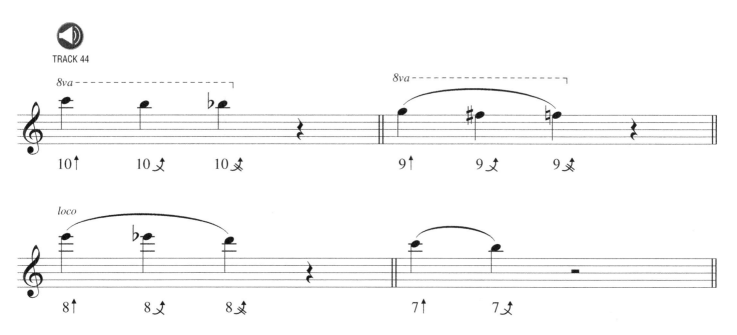

TRACK 44

The 7 hole will bend, but not an entire half step to B. The 8 and 9 holes also come up short when trying for another half step to D for the 8 hole, and F for the 9 hole. These are implied bends.

HIGH-NOTE EXERCISES

Here are a few high-note licks…

High-Note Triplet Lick

TRACK 45

High-Note Turnaround

TRACK 46

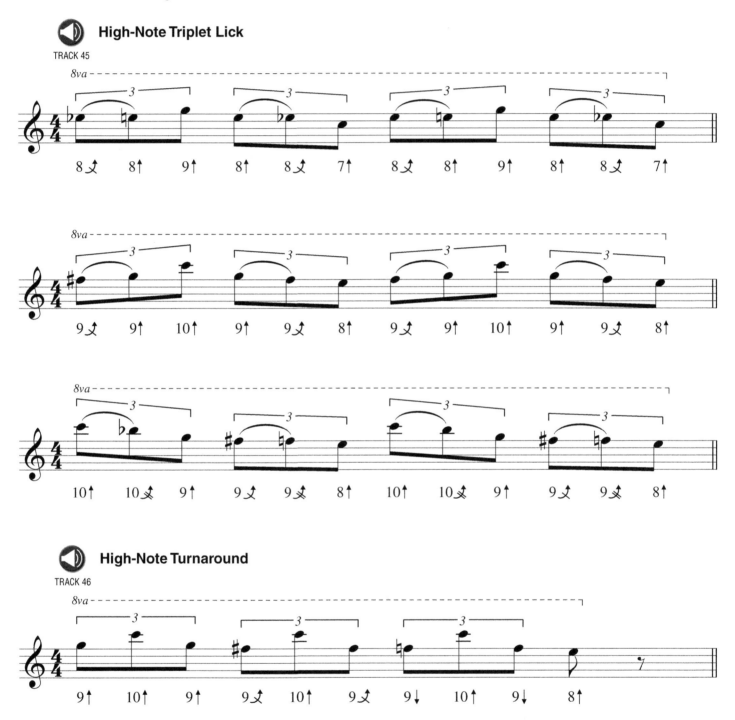

52 CHORDS AND OCTAVES

Another basic technique is developing the ability to play chords and octaves. Some of this is achieved with tongue blocking.

Octaves can be played all the way up the harp with blow notes. (An *octave* is two tones eight scale steps apart that have the same name—for example, hole-1 C and hole-4 C.) Your tongue covers the two holes between the holes you are playing, and the corners of your lips block the notes outside the notes you are playing.

Blow Octaves

TRACK 47

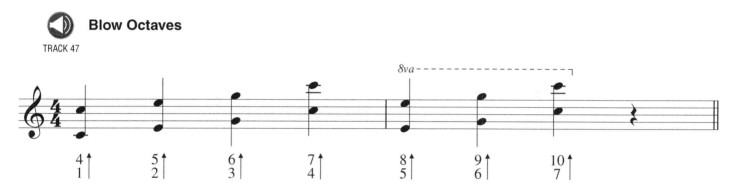

On the draw notes, holes 1 and 4 together create an octave. Holes 2 and 5 create the interval of a 7th, or a 7th chord with two notes missing. The next octaves change to a wider gap with three holes blocked out instead of two.

Draw Octaves and 7th

TRACK 48

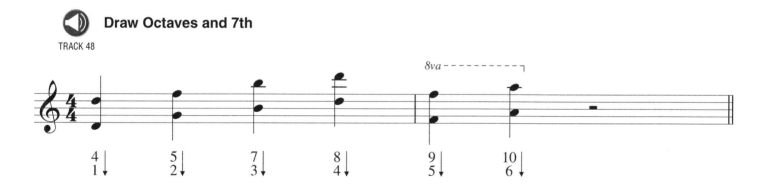

Playing two or more adjacent notes at the bottom of the harp forms major chords. On a C harp, drawing on holes 1, 2, and 3 at the same time produces a G major chord. Blowing on holes 1, 2, and 3 at the same time is a C major chord.

TRACK 49

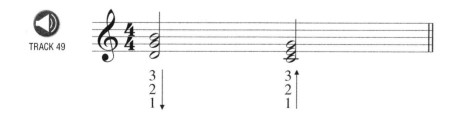

Try playing the two-note descending intervals exercise in Tip #49, using tongue blocking:

TRACK 50

53 GLISSANDO

A *glissando* is defined as a rapid slide through a series of consecutive tones in a scale-like passage. This is an important technique that makes good use of the close proximity of the holes. Glissandos (also called glisses) can help create continuity in a solo, and also gives the appearance of some fast playing. The idea is to slide up or down several notes before you settle on the target note at the end of a phrase. You could also start a phrase on a gliss, or play licks that are made up of all glisses. Here are some examples:

"Charge!"

TRACK 51

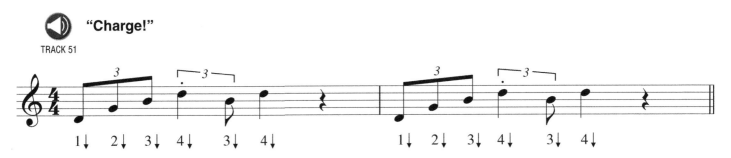

"Call to the Post"

TRACK 52

Triplet Descent

TRACK 53

54 VIBRATO

You can develop more character in your phrases by coloring notes with vibrato. *Vibrato* is a throbbing effect created by rapidly modulating the pitch. There are several types:

a. **Hand Wah:** When you are holding the harmonica, allow your hands to meet in front of the harp and create a seal. The tighter the seal, the more pronounced the wahs will be. When you are playing, you can open and close the seal at selected moments to create the vibrato known as hand wah. You can open and close quickly or slowly, depending on what kind of sound you are after. You can also fan with your right hand for that campfire sound.

TRACK 54

b. **Jaw Vibrato:** When you are holding a note, you can move your jaw up and down at whatever rate you wish, to create a vibrato effect.

TRACK 55

c. **Throat Vibrato:** While holding a note, you can make your Adams apple (or the female equivalent) go up and down. This will create vibrato.

TRACK 56

d. **Growl:** There's a rough-sounding vibrato that you can produce by growling (like Roy Orbison on "Pretty Woman") from the back of your throat.

TRACK 57

e. **Tongue Vibrato:** Removing your tongue repeatedly while playing a chord or octave creates another kind of vibrato.

TRACK 58

55 THE WARBLE, TRILL, OR SHAKE

Everyone has a different name for this, but it is a familiar harmonica sound. Start by drawing holes 4 and 5 as a chord. Then, holding the harp steadily, narrow the opening in your mouth and waggle your head back and forth to play the notes alternately instead of playing them together. You can change the rate of speed between waggles for different effects. You are not limited to doing this on holes 4 and 5. It can be done on any two adjacent notes, both blowing and drawing.

 Warble with Varied Speed

TRACK 59

A good way to gain control over this technique is to play Blues Lick #1 (Tip #7) using the warble on each note:

TRACK 60

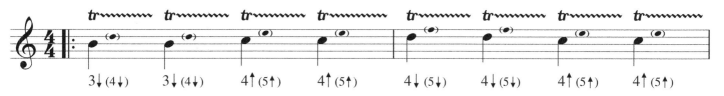

56 COMBINE TECHNIQUES

A great harp player has the ability to execute, improvise, and accompany tastefully. The ability to combine several techniques is the mark of an experienced player.

While playing the following combination exercises, consider adding different kinds of vibratos.

Incorporate bends into your trill:

TRACK 61

Incorporate trills into your octaves:

TRACK 62

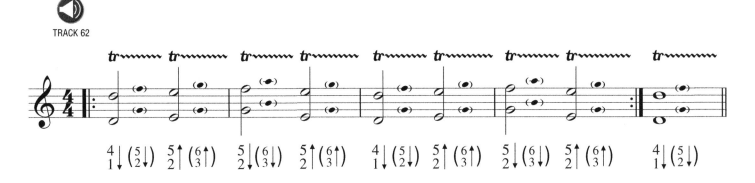

 DYNAMICS

Be aware of the volume (or *dynamics*) of your playing, and use it to musically color your notes and phrases. You wouldn't want to play with the same volume or intensity all night, or even all the way through any particular song or solo. Vary the intensity and volume of your notes and phrases to help bring your playing to life.

 MORE ABOUT BUILDING A SOLO

Think of soloing as telling a story. Build your solos like a conversation, or a five-course meal. Let your ideas out gradually, and slowly build in intensity. There should be a curve, so that your solo starts with something ear-catching, builds to a climax, then concludes with phrases that might relate to the whole structure. Employ dynamics. Leave some empty spaces. You don't have to fill up every beat, and your solo will be more interesting if you don't.

Some songs are more appropriate than others for stretching out and building a long solo. Some are less so. But either way, have a sense of economy. Simplicity really works. If you are noodling *ad infinitum*, it will likely get boring. Be tasteful and concise.

59 HARP MAINTENANCE

Clean your harps after use. A damp cloth lightly rubbed over all surfaces at the end of your session is adequate. Pat it dry, and either put it in the box that you bought it in, or put it to rest in whatever harp case you are using.

60 TOOL KIT

All your harps will eventually need some maintenance. Three tools you should own for this purpose are:

a. A **small screwdriver** (either Phillips or flat-head, depending on what kind of harps you play)

b. A **safety razor blade** (the kind of razor blade that has a handle on one side), or any small tool with a flat, thin edge for reed support

c. A **jeweler's file**—a small, sometimes three-sided file that can look like a tiny rasp

Usually, two screws fasten the covers onto your harmonica. They either set into female screws, or have a nut on the bottom. These are easily removed with the screwdriver.

Once the covers are removed, the exposed reeds are ready to be worked on.

61 JAMMED REEDS

Sometimes reeds will get jammed, blocked with debris, or go out of tune. These problems can be addressed. By playing, identify the reed that needs work by number, and whether it's a blow or draw. After removing the reed plate covers, inspect the reed that needs work. If the reed is jammed, sometimes just inspecting it will reveal a foreign object that can be removed.

Carefully slide your razor under the reed, pull up slightly, and then release it. By plucking the reed gently with the edge of the razor, it might be enough to free it up. You can also slide the razor under the reed and support it just above the reed plate, or even the edges of the hole that the reed sits in. Using the edge of your jeweler's file, lightly scrape the edges or body of the exposed reed. This can help clean up burrs, dirt, or whatever is jamming the reed.

TUNING

Reeds are thin strips of brass, and when they experience metal fatigue, they will go out of tune. Before the inner workings of the harmonica were revealed, we mostly discarded a harp even if only one of the 20 reeds was flat or jammed. Now we can make them last a little longer. The reeds that most often go out of tune are the ones that get bent a lot, namely 1–6 draw.

The draw reeds are riveted on the outside of the bottom plate. To correct a problem, first support the reed with the razor. If the reed has gone flat, you can use the jeweler's file to gently file away a little bit of the reed at the un-riveted end to raise the pitch. If a reed goes sharp, you file at the other riveted end. Be conservative, because if you go too far, it's hard to go back and adjust.

It is more difficult to work on the blow reeds, because they are set inside the reed plate, but you can gently push the reed out with the end of the screwdriver, catch it with your razor blade, and then try tuning while the reed is supported by the razor. Some harps have reed plates that can be removed by taking out the screws. Removing the blow plate makes it easier to work on blow reeds.

To check your tuning after filing, you can gently pluck the reed and listen to determine if the pitch has moved to where you intended. If not, file a little more. Playing notes into a tuner is a good method to check tuning. The better the tuner, the more accurate the tuning will be. With or without a tuner, it's good to check a reed that you've just worked on against a higher or lower octave on the same instrument. Just by playing the harmonica, your ear will tell you if the reeds are in tune. You can test the harmonica by holding the covers in place without screwing them back on.

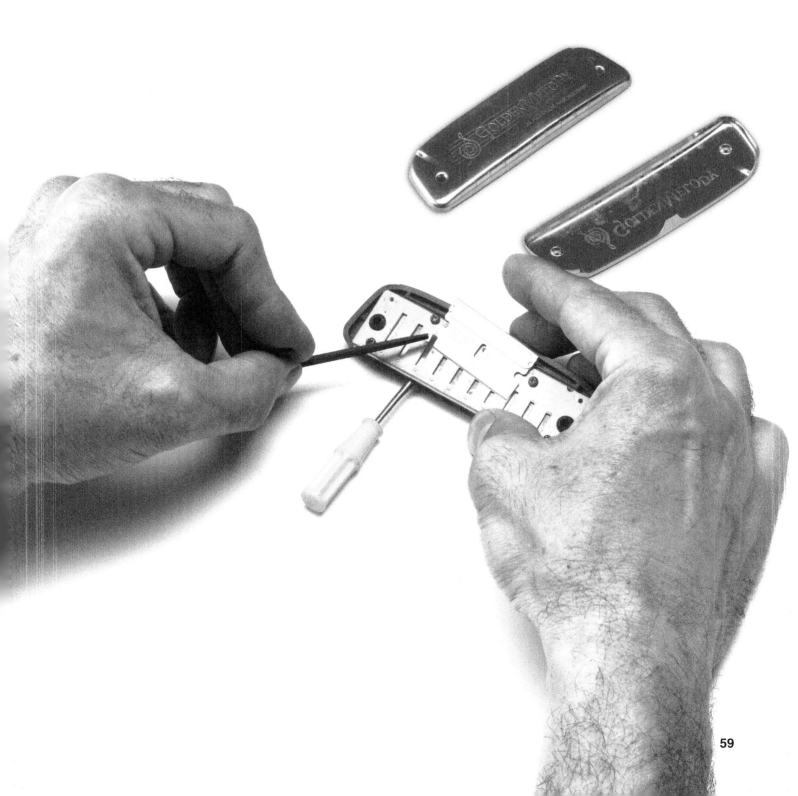

 63 REED SET-UP

Sometimes a reed will stick just because it's sitting too low in the reed plate. You can correct this problem and also set your reeds up for easier playing by gapping them. Ideally, you want the un-riveted ends of the reeds to sit just barely above the reed plate. If it is sitting too low, you can slide the razor blade under the reed and exert a little smooth pressure to raise the reed just a tiny bit. Different gaps make the reeds respond differently.

 64 FINAL CLEAN UP

Before re-assembling a harp that I've been working on, I run my file over the front edge of the reed plate covers and also the slots that the covers sit in on the plates. This cleans them up and the result is a tighter instrument that will play better.

If there is dirt or rust anywhere on the inner surfaces of the covers, and there will be, this would be a good time to clean those up, too.

It would be smart to experiment with these techniques on an old, retired harp before working on your good ones.

Finally, save your old unfixable harps for parts. Sometimes you can switch out a whole reed plate, or re-use a cover.

65 HARP CASES

Harmonicas are fairly small and we usually need to carry several of them, so a good carrying case is helpful. Think through what you will need in your harp case.

Several harp manufacturers now produce designated harp cases. Some are hard shell cases made of plastic, metal, or canvas. Some have foam with cutouts to in-set your harps. One characteristic that differs about them is how many harps they will hold. Before you settle on a case, think about out how many harps you use on a regular basis.

I have found old photographic slide carrying cases made of metal, usually at rummage sales. After removing the slide divider, I put a thin sheet of foam in the bottom and then insert the top tray from a tackle box that has dividers. The top tray from a model 420 Plano tackle box is the perfect size for me. By cutting out certain parts of the plastic divider, I create an organized system that holds up to 25 harmonicas in a compact case.

The harp case fits in my gig bag with my microphones and cords. My repair kit also fits into this case. I carry song lists, contracts, or other paperwork in the lid. I also have a soft cloth that I lay over the top of my harps for added protection. Sometimes I will lay the cloth between the case and whatever surface I lay my case on at venues to prevent it from sliding around. There are few things worse than to have your harp case vibrate off your amp and scatter your harps onto the floor. When you're playing an outdoor gig in the hot sun, you can lay your cloth over the harps you aren't using to keep them from getting too hot to the touch.

I have other cases that hold a smaller number of harps if I'm off to a jam, or some gig where I'll only need a few. I find that carrying seven harps is usually adequate for most jams or sit-ins. Those seven are: A, B♭, C, D, E♭, F, and G. Other times, I'll use a case that holds twelve harps so that I'm ready for any key. Occasionally, I'll show up at a jam with just one or two.

I always have a couple of loose harps in my car to play along with the radio, or to work out ideas at red lights.

66 HARP KEY MARKERS

You'll need to know which harp is which in your case. I often switch harps during songs, so it's critical for me to have a system for identifying them on the fly. One method is to put the sticker that came with the box on the back of the harp—if there is a sticker. You can overlay a piece of transparent tape over it to prevent your hands from rubbing it off.

Lately, I've been using an automotive touch-up paint pen on the back of my harps instead of the stickers. The paint never rubs off.

67 AMPLIFIERS IN GENERAL

There are many philosophies about amplifying and amending the harmonica sound. I once heard of a famous harp player asked about his choice of amplifier. His reply was, "It makes it louder." Ok…

There are numerous options, and experimentation will be helpful. It's good, clean fun to go to a music store and try out different combinations of microphones and amps. If you have a mic you like, bring it along to the store to try with different amps. Since the salesman wants to sell you this equipment, he will likely be accommodating. Try different mics, too.

68 AMPLIFIER TYPES

There is little in a used amplifier that can't be fixed, so consider buying a used amp. Some players think a tube amp, especially a vintage tube amp, gives the best sound. It is true that tube amps do usually sound a little warmer if set up properly, but, whatever amp gives you the sound you're after… that's the right amp. Either solid state or tube amps can all be fine. There are now several harp amps available on the market specifically designed for amplifying harmonica.

Little Walter, the guy most responsible for the amplified harp sound as we know it, changed amps and microphones like he changed his socks, so don't feel like you can't have several, or can't make a change occasionally.

69 AMPLIFIER SIZE

Consider the size of the venues you usually play in. Many tube amplifiers need to be turned up loud to get a good sound. If you have a big amp, most clubs will be too small to turn it up. Something smaller might be more appropriate for most gigs, and if you're playing on a big stage, they'll be putting a microphone in front your amp anyway. You might want to own different sized amps for different rooms. Amps have different sizes and number of speakers, which also affects how they sound. Experiment.

DEALING WITH FEEDBACK

70 AMPLIFIER PLACEMENT

For purposes of eliminating feedback, hearing yourself better, or getting a better ensemble sound, consider where you physically place your amplifier. You may want to elevate it on a chair, or lean it back if it has legs, or even face it toward the wall. You can also affect the sound by covering the back if it's an open-backed amp.

71 DEALING WITH FEEDBACK

When trying to play as loud as the band while using a hand-held harp microphone, you can experience feedback problems. Try changing your EQ, either with the amp's tone knobs or an EQ pedal. Moving away from your amplifier can help. Often the response of the mic is the culprit, so try using a different mic. Your playing will not be appreciated if your mic is squealing with feedback.

There are many options for hand-held microphones. Things to consider when trying mics:

a. **Comfort:** How the mic feels in your hands with a harp in front of it is important.

b. **On/Off Switch or Volume Control:** It can be helpful to have a mic with an on/off switch or a volume control. If you settle on a mic that doesn't have these, you can find a local electronics person to build a volume control into your mic. A volume pedal is another answer.

c. **Tone:** Different mics come with their own particular tone, but there are infinite ways to adjust the tone of a mic, be it with EQ, amplifier controls, effects pedals, or switching elements.

d. **All of the Above:** I once interviewed a famous harp player who knew Little Walter, and I asked him about Walter's tone. Was it his amp? His mic? His answer: "It was the way he played." Balance your mic, your amp, and the way you play for the sound you want.

e. **Brands:** The most widely used harp mics are the Astatic JT-30 and the Shure Green Bullet. Production of the Astatic never stopped, and they now make one with a volume control. The Green Bullet used to be a fairly rare item, but Shure has re-issued them. You can also use a Shure SM-57 or SM-58, or any other mic that provides a good sound and feel for your tastes. There are now mics specifically designed for getting good harmonica tone. Search the web or your local music store.

Some harp microphones contain an element or cartridge that can be changed out with a screwdriver and a soldering gun. You might have a mic with a sound you like, but is unwieldy. One can usually remove the element and install it in a mic with a better feel. Interestingly, I've seen accordions with Astatic cartridges in them. Amplifiers designed for accordion often make good harp amps.

Controlled-Magnetic TRANSDUCER
SHURE BROTHERS INC,
Mfd. under Shure Patents
2,454,425
MADE IN U.S.A.
MODEL NUMBER
99C86 RH

Some harp microphones have built-in cords, like the old Green Bullet. These tend to break at the worst possible time, so if you are committed to a mic that came with a built-in chord, you might consider having your technician install a female phono jack. Then you can use the guitar cord of your choice.

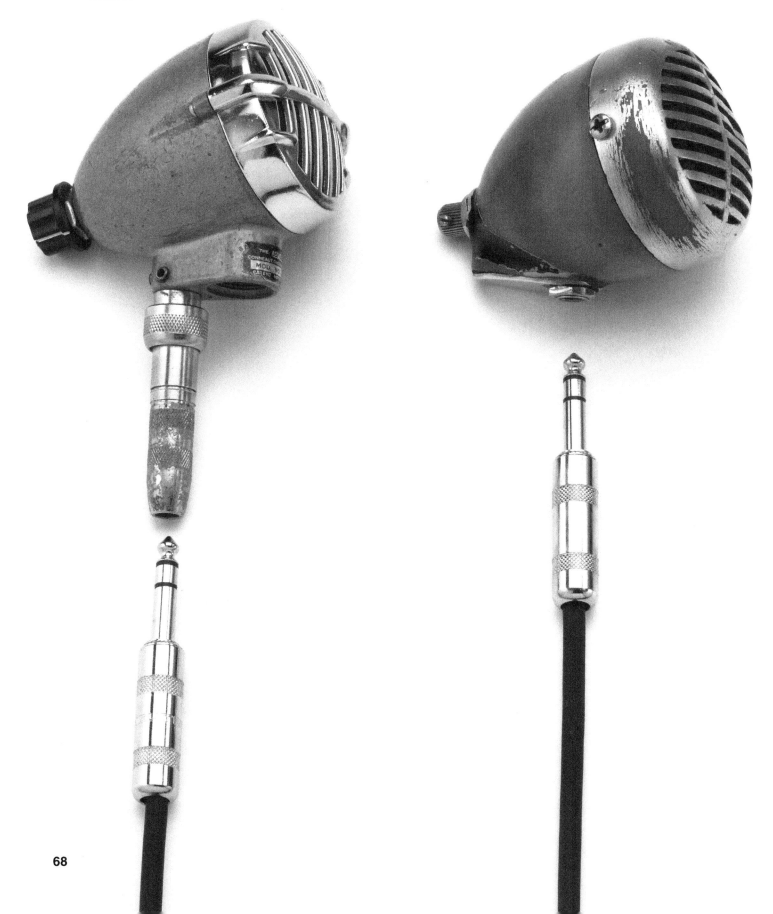

75 FIND GOOD MAINTENANCE PEOPLE

Mics go down, as do amps and pedals. Develop a good relationship with a repairman so you can get your work done quickly, confidently, and at a reasonable price. There are also harmonica repairmen.

76 EFFECTS PEDALS

It can get monotonous to play with the same tone all night. Other instruments employ different electronic effects. Why not harp? Try out different pedals. You may want to buy a reverb, echo, or delay pedal, even if your amp has reverb.

If your amp is pretty clean sounding and you want a little distortion, there are dozens of pedals on the market that will give you infinite combinations of clean or dirty boost and distortion (a good thing for a big amp in a small room). An octave pedal can give your sound a little more girth, or lean it toward that of a saxophone. A chorus pedal is handy for emulating organ tones and making your washes more effective. You may want to leave some pedals on all night, like distortion. Others are good for particular spots, but don't overdo it. Flangers, phase shifters, wah wah pedals, and a myriad of other effects are all worth experimenting with. But remember, if you aren't playing well, no amount of effects will hide it.

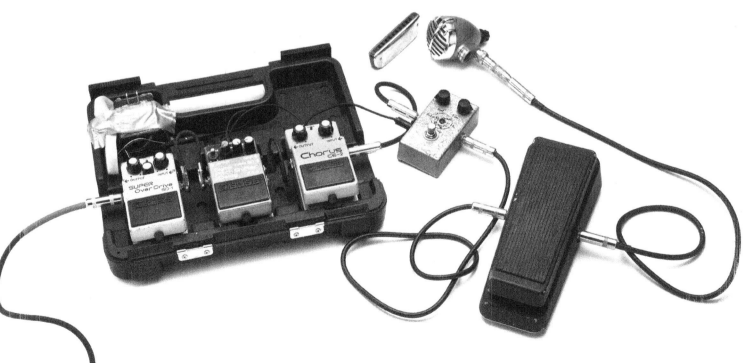

77 VOCAL MIC TECHNIQUE

Even if you aren't a singer, it's good to set up a vocal microphone on a stand for a clean sound. On some songs and in some genres it is more appropriate to have a clean acoustic harp sound. That's the time to play directly through a vocal mic. Without cupping a mic in your hands, it's possible to use a subtle hand-wah vibrato that you just can't get with a distorted amplified sound. In the low-volume spots of a ballad, you can really milk the vocal quality of the harmonica with hand wah. Sonny Boy Williamson II is a good example of a player who got a wide variety of rich tones without cupping the mic.

TRACK 63

78 HARP MIC TECHNIQUE

On some songs and styles, it's appropriate to pick up your designated harp mic and play with an electric sound. When you're cupping the mic, you can release a little bit of that compressed air to alter your tone, similar to the hand-wah technique. With some mics, blowing harder produces more distortion.

TRACK 64

When you're heading out to play a gig or a session, there are several items that you should have with you…

HARPS

Carry some extra harps. If there are certain keys that you play a lot, bring spares. A reed can fail at any time, and without a spare, you may be unable to play in certain keys without some compromise. The blues ensembles that I perform with often play in the keys of E, G, and A. Since I most often play in 2nd position, I always have a spare A, C, and D. If you play for recording sessions, bring a complete extra set along if you have them, as well as any special harps. Be prepared for anything!

There may be occasions when your only recourse to play in a certain key will be to fix your harp on the fly or at the break. Have your repair kit with you at gigs.

MICROPHONES

If you play with a harp microphone, consider getting a spare and keep it in your gig bag. If you're having feedback problems in a particular venue, using a different mic might be the solution. Your mic could also break. My gig bag always has at least three mics in it.

Extra microphone cords should also be part of the deal. If you pack a mic on a stand, you should consider having a spare mic clip. A little thing like a broken mic clip can really impair your ability to perform well. There's always gaffer's tape…

81 CORDS & MISCELLANEOUS ITEMS

If you use a harp microphone with a detachable cord, you'll want to have a spare cord. The same goes for carrying extra patch cords if you use effects. It's good to have an extension cord.

If you use multiple effects pedals, it's good to have an extra daisy chain, an extra nine-volt battery or two, and even a spare AC adapter. It's also good to have some fuses for your amplifier. If you use a tube amp, having extra power tubes can be good. If it's a heavy amp, you may want to invest in an appropriately-sized hand truck to save wear and tear on the amp and your back.

82 CHECKLIST

I bring different gear to different gigs. On some gigs, I need to bring harp gear, guitar gear, and PA gear, as well as CDs, promotional items, email list sign-ups, etc. It's easy to forget one of the million things you'll need, so a checklist is a good idea.

83 BUSINESS CARDS

You never know when someone might want to hire you for another gig, or get in touch with you for an interview or a lesson. Carry business cards. You might also want to have your date book with you. A printed calendar of upcoming performances with a web address or phone number is a good item to have available for interested fans.

HARP RACKS

Some harp players who also play guitar like to play them simultaneously. There are several harp holders available on the market. If you look at historical photos, you can see that some guys made them out of coat hangers and other materials. Jimmy Reed and Slim Harpo were both rack players, as are Bob Dylan and Neil Young.

When I use a rack, my technique involves putting a foot on the base of the microphone stand and pushing the harp right against the mic. This prevents the rack from swinging open when I push to play. This technique works best on a straight stand. Using a boom stand defeats the purpose of stabilizing the stand with your foot. Also, putting a wind screen on your mic is a good way to eliminate unwanted bumping noises.

JAM SESSIONS

It's important to practice around the house, but you are learning so that you can play with other people. Playing at jams is a great way to get some onstage experience. Playing in public sounds and feels different than it does in your basement. Jams are good places to meet, hear, and play with potential band mates, too. The 12-bar blues form is a common language at many jams. Get to know it well.

BE ARTICULATE

Learn the language needed to explain what you want other musicians to play. It's important to be able to spell out the rhythm pattern (Texas shuffle, flat tire, swing, slow blues, funk, two-feel, mojo beat, etc.), and chord changes (12-bar from the top, from the V, from the turnaround, quick change, ii–V turnaround, etc.), as well as whether to play solo sections differently from the main pattern. Don't forget reminders about how you want the song to begin or end if you have something in mind.

87 ON-STAGE LANGUAGE & SIGNALS

Different people use different signals on stage. Learn the language, and be alert. Ask the bandleader what signals he or she likes to use before the gig begins if you aren't sure. Adopt some language for those times you are leading the ensemble.

- A raised hand coming down quickly can mean a stop.

- When cueing chord changes to band members on stage, often the first finger held in the air indicates the I chord.

- Four fingers extended with the thumb folded over can mean IV chord.

- Thumb and fingers extended can mean the V chord.

- A hand brought down slowly can mean a quieter dynamic level of playing.

- A hand waving horizontally at the end of a song can mean to hold out the final flourish.

- Sometimes a hand with all fingers extended pushing toward you can mean a $5 fine for making a mistake.

- "Quick change" means the progression goes to the IV chord in the second bar.

- "From the turnaround" means the song starts in the 11th bar just before bouncing back to the V chord.

- "From the five," or the "third change" means to start on the V chord.

- "A button" means a final accent at the end of a song, usually cued by the drummer—if there is a drummer.

88 COUNT-OFFS—IMPORTANT!

If you are counting a song off, first take a minute to visualize where you want the tempo to land. Tempo is critical as to whether the song hits the groove or not. Once the band comes in, the tempo will be locked even if you counted it off too fast or too slow.

 89 FIND YOUR LEVEL

Some of the people you play with will be more skilled or more experienced than you. Some will be less so. You can tell when you hit the stage who's who. Playing with better players can elevate your playing through a kind of osmosis, and if you are the better player, sometimes you can pull the other musicians up a notch.

 90 RELAX AND FIND THE GROOVE

Whether playing solo, duo, or with a larger ensemble, try to find the intangible element known as "the groove." Everybody on stage needs to be on the same page regarding tempo, feel, dynamics, and communication. A great band is in the groove all night.

It's not easy to play well if you are uptight. Find a way to relax onstage, and you will be amazed at how much better you will perform.

 91 KEEPING TIME

Develop the habit of tapping your foot, or find some physical way to help you keep time while playing. You want this to become second nature. It can help to practice with a metronome.

 92 GO HEAR OTHER PLAYERS

Go out and listen to both local and touring players. This is as important as listening to recorded music. When I was starting to play, a world-class blues harpist played regularly in my own town. Jim Liban raised the bar high for all the aspiring harp players in my area. His great musical ideas and onstage theatrics gave me loads of inspiration. I might not have realized the possibilities of the harmonica had I not heard Jim when I was starting out.

 93 POINTS OF PROFESSIONALISM

If you want to be a working harp player, be available for gigs, and be easy to reach. Return phone calls and emails promptly.

Show up for gigs with enough time to get ready comfortably, and be punctual.

 94 BE ALERT ON STAGE

Whether you are the bandleader or a sideman, good communication is critical. Blues music is very spontaneous. Many arrangements are improvised on stage, so be alert with your eyes and ears.

 95 MONITORS

If there are monitor speakers on stage, know what to tell the technician that you want to hear. It's most important to hear your harmonica and the vocals, as the vocals often contain arrangement cues. If all you hear is guitar, drums, or bass, you're going to have trouble playing well. Also, don't have an attitude with front-of-house or monitor guys. Sound technicians are there to make you sound good, and they should be your best friends.

On most club dates, your amp will be your monitor. Be sure to place it in such a way that you can hear yourself. Even if there are monitors, hearing your amp directly on stage is usually preferable.

 96 TALK TO THE AUDIENCE

An audience is not usually made up of musicians. It is comprised of people who are assessing how you look, how you act, and how you express your identity on stage, so project your personality. Have some jokes and patter ready between songs. Introduce the band. Get ready to deal with hecklers. These are all practical matters that have little to do with how you play, but have everything to do with how you go over. You are selling your personality as much as you are playing music.

97 DEVELOP SOME SHTICK

It can be boring to watch a band that just stands there. Find some natural body movements that help you accent the music. Don't be afraid to move around a little.

Develop some shtick to have in your arsenal. Things like walking on the bar while you play, or learn to lean against a wall and play while standing on your head, or jump on a table while you're playing. Sit on the lap of an audience member, or use a wireless mic and walk through the audience. I once left a club while playing and hopped on a bus! These are the things that likely will be better remembered than your playing.

98 PROMOTE YOURSELF

Whether you are promoting yourself individually or as part of an ensemble, develop a press kit. This can include a picture, a bio, a song list, general descriptive information, contact information, reviews, references, and music samples.

It's also good to have a web site to which you can send fans and buyers. Many local newspapers and some radio stations offer free calendar listings. Take advantage of them. If people don't know you're playing, they can't come and hear you.

99 WHO'S THE LEADER?

It would be nice if you could just show up for gigs and play, but if you're in a band, someone has to take care of business. Some folks are just naturally good at these important tasks. The list of tasks is long, and he who does these things often goes unappreciated. Scheduling rehearsals, selecting material, finding and booking jobs, promoting public appearances, organizing promotional materials (which can include graphic art layout and duplication, as well as making and mailing posters, among other things), creating set lists, mailing lists, getting paid and paying out, doing accounting, which can include 1099s and other tax forms, and a myriad of other tasks all need to get done. Perhaps splitting up the tasks is a good approach.

100 OTHER KINDS OF HARMONICAS

Beyond the 10-hole diatonic harmonica, there are also other kinds of harps. They are in two categories:

a. **Chromatic Harps:** Chromatic harmonicas have a single set of holes, but a double set of reeds. There is a push button mechanism on the side of the harp that accesses the extra reeds and makes the chromatic scale available, but without bends or overblows. It does have some bending capacity, but not as much as a diatonic. I think of it as an entirely different instrument as one has to play it with a more sensitive attack, it has a distinctly different sound, and it requires learning a different set of hole-to-note relationships.

b. **Tremolo Harps:** Tremolo harps have a double row of holes set on top of each other. There is a tremolo effect, but there is virtually no likelihood of increasing the chromatic possibilities by bending. Its practical applications are limited, though it does sound nice on some campfire and folk songs.

101 A FEW DON'TS

Don't be the guy in the audience that is playing harmonica along with the band. You may think that your contribution is being appreciated, but it is not.

Don't soak your harps in water, whiskey, or anything else. It will ruin them.

Refrain from eating before you play. This can cause reed malfunction. Drinking sticky liquids can also gum up your harps.

HARMONICA NOTATION LEGEND

Harmonica music can be notated two different ways: on a *musical staff*, and in *tablature*.

THE MUSICAL STAFF shows pitches and rhythms and is divided by bar lines into measures. Pitches are named after the first seven letters of the alphabet.

TABLATURE graphically represents the harmonica music. Each note will be accompanied by a number, 1 through 10, indicating what hole you are to play. The arrow that follows indicates whether to blow or draw. (All examples are shown using a C diatonic harmonica.)

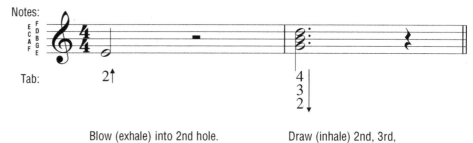

Blow (exhale) into 2nd hole.

Draw (inhale) 2nd, 3rd, & 4th holes together.

Notes on the C Harmonica

Exhaled (Blown) Notes

Inhaled (Drawn) Notes

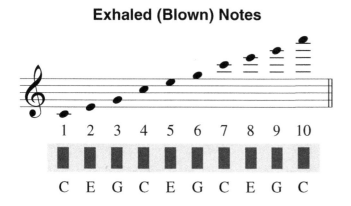

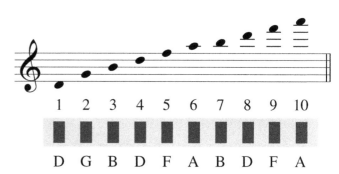

Bends

Blow Bends		**Draw Bends**	
	• 1/4 step		• 1/4 step
	• 1/2 step		• 1/2 step
	• 1 step		• 1 step
	• 1 1/2 steps		• 1 1/2 steps